The Erasmus Foundation

Treatise on Education

Paddina Cole

Ruscora Publishing

COPYRIGHT © THE ERASMUS FOUNDATION 2020

All rights in this book are reserved and no part thereof may be used or reproduced without written permission of

The Erasmus Foundation
Moat House
Banyards Green
Laxfield
Woodbridge
Suffolk
IP13 8ER
United Kingdom
Tel: +44 (0) 1986 798682
admin@erasmus-foundation.org
www.erasmus-foundation.org

Registered Charity No. 281458

ISBN 9780954906795

Published in 2020 by Ruscora Publishing

CONTENTS

Introduction	1
The Present State of Education	5
The Future of Education	9
The Balanced Child	17
Seven Ages of Man	22

INTRODUCTION

"Real education should educate us out of self into something far finer; into a selflessness which links us with all humanity."

Nancy Astor

It is widely accepted within the World at this time that the education system, especially amongst young children at primary school age, is struggling, whilst teachers are finding it very stressful and difficult to manage. Equally so, young children are suffering the results of stress and anxieties which should never occur amongst people so young. Bullying is still a major concern, as are the increasing amount of mental health issues which, again, are unacceptable, especially with such a young age group.

This treatise, dictated by spirit at The Erasmus Foundation, is offered as an alternative method of teaching which has been used in past civilisations to great success, and following this, it should be recognised that every child is an individual and every individual's life is pre-planned, tapestried and determined mostly how a young person is to develop and mature with a single purpose in their life. It is, therefore, difficult for some children who are forced to acclimatise to a generalised system that dictates how they should be, regardless of their very structured make up which does not comply with the expectations of the general educational system.

It must be recognised that each and every individual Tapestry has a purpose for a meaningful life for that individual, and one of the most important aspects of a child's education should be focussing on understanding the individual's purpose and meaning in life. Further to this, children should be allowed to explore life and be encouraged to learn the basic spiritual values of life which must include good communication, graciousness and concern for others. Why is it necessary to overload children of a young age with academic subjects under a great deal of stress, to force them to learn these subjects which may be of no purpose in their future life?

Is it not better, as in previous civilisations, that the basic values of life are taught at a very young age, without any stress, until the age of 9 or 10, when academic subjects are then introduced and children can choose the subject of their interest which would relate to them as an individual, anticipating the direction of their careers and interest for future life? How many of us have been forced to learn subjects at school that have not related in any way to our own purpose and direction within our life; and furthermore, what is the point of forcing this cruel routine of education upon such young, vulnerable minds to cause stress and mental imbalance, while simple, basic values and behaviour are ignored, promoting children to grow up in an ever increasing unbalanced World?

"Very importantly, education should be there to help children understand themselves, why they are in life here on the Earth and, if it is possible, to discover their true purpose and meaning for their life."

Paddina Cole

The Present State of Education

(From a lecture by the spirit of Paddina 1st May 2020)

The subject we are to discuss is the present state of education in your country and perhaps to a degree it is common place throughout your World although some countries do have different methods, it must be said. But, I wanted to really present to you a little of the negative aspects of your form of education at present and I think this is widely understood and accepted that something is not quite right which is proved by the increase in mental disorders and disruptive behaviour of young children. Further to this, it would seem that the levels of stress and anxiety amongst young children is increasing where this should not be so, ever. So, why is this?

Of course, making demands on young brains, as developing as they are within these young forms, is destructive, damaging to cause this much stress and anxiety by imposing exams and tests which have been introduced in, I gather, more recent years. Furthermore, it is not spiritually correct to make demands and impose these things on anyone. Spirit do not behave in this manner and in my land there is no demand whatsoever, no pressure, no stress. This would be quite out of place in spirit and really does not exist in spirit. So, why should it exist on the Earth, especially by the way of damaging such small, developing brains? It is not right.

There is also a lack of good, or should I say, proper communication amongst the young children and their tutors. The teachers have been given a strict code of teaching they must abide to according to a curriculum which has been designed and put in place with authority by the Ministry of Education and everyone has to follow this according to the rules. The consequence of this is that teachers are under pressure to show and exhibit levels of improvement, qualifications, standards, all of these, which are then to be monitored and reviewed by the educational authorities. Sometimes, demands of the system require that the teachers do not have sufficient time and space to accommodate all that is necessary for the skill of teaching correctly. One failing of this is that individual children are not being given sufficient attention, concern and time allowed for them to perhaps identify particular problems or situations within a class which would then create further problems for the developing children. The consequence of this, as it is beginning to be realised, is one of the causes of the increase in mental instability within children.

Also, with problems such as bullying, generally

speaking, it would seem that this particular issue exists still quite widely and has not been resolved as it should have been. Why is this? Is it, again, that the teachers are under too much pressure and do not have the time to resolve individual issues like this? But, unfortunately, some situations like this within a group of young children can be widely impactive and damaging to more than just a few children in the class. It is also then beyond the control of the teachers to maintain discipline, as some children have been known to be so disruptive that they are really in control and this should not be so, not at all.

There are basic principles and values in spirit which are ignored within education on the Earth, some of which, in the past, were taught and given value and thought to be necessary for a young child's education, but not so today. But it is the lack of these values, basic principles, which must be part of a child's life, and extremely important if a child is to mature and develop in a balanced way. So, without these principles, it is not too hard to understand why the system is failing. How is this all going to end?

Now, given the situation of your World and this virus pandemic, schools have been closed and I would suggest in the future will not reopen in the way they have performed in the past. It would be inappropriate with all the changes that are expected to happen within the next months and years. So, your educational system has to be reviewed, reconsidered and, I put it, that it really needs a revolution, which is what is going to happen.

One thing is for sure; your World needs a new education. It needs spiritual tuition throughout your World to develop Mankind in a way which will then allow him to develop and grow spiritually. It is necessary. It is a requirement. All that is going on in your World at this time is part of the master plan of The Great Mind who has tapestried all this to happen for good reason.

Because your World is so materialistic, all the education system aims to do is to make people fit to serve within the materialistic world and that future. So, what is measured is the success of the ability of someone to fit well in your nation to then provide the opportunities and facilities to make good commerce and sales across to other nations. And if you consider this, is that not simply the aims of your educational system which has no regard for the individual, their difficulties in life that some have and, more importantly, how they are structured, some of whom are extremely out of balance? This system is not aimed to help, support and benefit people; it is there only to form the basis of a new generation of materialists.

The Future of Education

(From a lecture by the spirit of Paddina 10th April 2020)

The subject is for forthcoming education in your World. How it is at present is not suitable for the young, or for anyone, and this is recognised, I would suggest, by most people, including those who are responsible for designing and putting into place the educational system and its curriculum at present, not knowing really any alternative other than that which history has provided for. Everything that has been designed for educating young children has been based on previous experiences and has not always shown to work but, nevertheless, those responsible have chosen to continue with their tunnelled vision, may I say, for lack of appreciating any alternative.

This is to change, it has shown in recent times not to work completely, causing stress and some mental disorders within schools and that is not right, surely. So, we must progress with what we believe here is a good, sound, healthy curriculum, if you wish to call it this, for the future. I think we should find an alternative word to this word '*curriculum*' because that belongs to an academic meaning, whereas what we are proposing are the basic values for life which surely must be learnt at an early age when children are beginning to communicate, beginning to find the World of interest and wishing to learn. But, above all, it requires as soon as children start to communicate that they should be learning the most basic values of life very simply, and in a way which children would want to adopt naturally with pleasure, with curiosity, with a desire to perform well and to really impress their tutors and family, and friends and neighbours, whoever. One cannot force education on anyone, it is not possible. People have tried but it requires that the person receiving information must absorb it within their brain sufficiently well to memorise it, to take it in, and use that accordingly. That is not possible if people are forced to learn. So it should be that the approach is offered. It is a gift. It is something worthwhile that any child, or anyone, would appreciate its value and, therefore, if it is offered in the correct way, then it would be received and welcomed happily and, one would hope, joyfully.

So, this is the approach for the future. That is the starting point. But, accordingly, this is going to require teachers to be taught. Teachers will have to learn new skills, knowledge and understanding and, again, they will be seen really more as advisers, people with knowledge and skills who the children would wish to approach for their learning, for knowledge, and this would be shared amongst all children. Today there will be children who do not wish to learn, who would rather go out and play, do whatever they want to do but refuse to learn, and it is very challenging for any teacher to impress that child with knowledge in a way which they would find acceptable. So, if there is a child that refuses to join in, accept what is being offered, then so be it. There must come a time when that child has exhausted all that he or she wishes to do in play, fulfilled all his or her needs to enjoy these toys or whatever they choose, and then they will be most keen to find out what all their friends are learning and gaining by it. Does he or she want to be left behind and not have the benefit of learning wisdom and being given knowledge? No. So, it is a bit like fishing, you have to use a bait to draw the attention, and when it is seen as wholesome and nutritious then that child will take interest and want to learn, as it is right that they would.

So, this doesn't require any form of examinations or testing or anything stressful such as this. When a child is learning the basics of life, learning how life should be, how they should enjoy life, it doesn't require to be tested. It requires that children then reveal what they are learning by how they are, by their behaviour, how they are adopting manners and behaviour which is correct and balanced; and what they say will indicate this clearly. So, if some children are making headway more than others, again, that is natural, and that is normal, as it should be, as everyone is an individual.

Every child is an individual, but there may be some who are perhaps finding it difficult, then it is the responsibility of all of those involved offering this teaching that they should then enquire further to see what has caused the child to lose interest, or not gain interest to begin with. This is how it should be, and every single child as an individual is important and must be heard and seen and responded to without question.

So, the teaching that is offered will be very simple, it will be very straightforward. It will be offered more in discussion, in questioning where a group of children will be with, let us say, a tutor, or more than one tutor, and together they will learn from each other and the development of teaching will grow. And it might involve some of the activities already practised in schools but without the pressure, without the stress, and without having to learn facts and figures and hard academic subjects for this young age; only to be introduced at a later time when the children have matured to an age well balanced, ready then to absorb academic learning with the interest and desire to learn that a young, developing mind would normally and very naturally have. That is how it has to be.

Now, in the past, in some very ancient civilisations, going back, it was the priesthood who were responsible for tutoring, and even in your times, going back a few hundred years, it was the monasteries and the nunneries who were, let us say, the universities of their time, where people were taught academic subjects. Yes, again, not so pressurised as today, but nonetheless it was skilfully learnt and taught. But because these were institutions of a religion, whether Christianity or not, other places had similar structures in Islam, as an example, but because these universities were based in religion then certain values were naturally taught and were accepted as ways of life. So, where some monasteries were kept very quiet, again their manners, their behaviour was very naturally gracious one to the other, and this became just part of that normal way of life, and was seen as to be balanced and aspiring to spiritual behaviour and acceptance. And that is how it will be more in the future. It will come eventually, in time, that so much of this won't have to be deliberately taught, it will be widely known and people will behave accordingly. Only if they are in error would it become necessary then to make a point of teaching, of tutoring to correct a student, no matter how young or mature they may be. And that has to follow.

Above all, there should be no punishment. How can there be? The Great Mind does not punish. He offers facilities for his children to learn, coming to the University of Life, Eritha, the Earth. He provides the opportunity, the Tapestry of Life, for every one of his spirits to come to the Earth, to live a life, and to learn by it, regardless of the outcome. There is no pressure, there is no stress involved other than that within the life, of course, but spiritually there is no punishment, as you all know. It simply is an opportunity to learn and develop yourself. And that is how young children will be encouraged to learn, by this means. And if a whole class-room of children reject what is offered and would rather go out and play and do other things, then so be it. There must not be such strong rules and regulations as required by the laws of your land, and other countries the same. It must be free will and it will be free will because those who naturally, as a child, have an instinctive desire to want to learn, will, if the substance of the mental food they are offered is nutritious, tasteful and wholesome; they will want a part of it, they will want to learn, and this is how it will be taught.

In the priesthood, in pre-Ancient Egypt, where children were taught, if the Priest wasn't accepted or felt that he had nothing to offer the children, then he would remain silent; if this should happen. But, in truth, it never did because the Priests had a wisdom, had knowledge, and all wanted to learn and just have a little bit of what they could learn from the Priest; very, very simple.

So, again, activities to be considered: discipline, really in a way it should not be necessary. It will not be necessary. If a child is rude, badly behaved, then they will be told so, correctly, openly, in truth, in front of everybody. That should be enough to resolve any problem. There are some children who could be disruptive, of course, who perhaps have certain qualities which are going to make them a little difficult to handle. This then has to be approached, again, with tutoring for the tutor, with spiritual understanding and appreciation. These matters will be dealt with in the right way. But discipline should not be a word that could be used or should be used in the educational system of the future. This will be something of the past.

Any further questions, or points of discussion, will be dealt with in the future, when we might talk about what subjects and what will be learnt, and how it will be learnt. And we will discuss this at a later time. Just to say, at this point, that above all, the Natural Law is the Law that will be followed; no other. Therefore, it will be important for children to learn about nature as well. Of course, this is not going to interest all individuals. Some are going to prefer other activities, and other interests, and that is right. But everything will be maintained according to the Natural Law, and that is the important significance; that will be the basis of teaching for the future.

Children instinctively, intuitively, have an enquiring mind, and all you have to do is provide them with the opportunity to explore the natural world. It is there. It is on offer. If all people were to do this with the time and freedom to explore nature, this civilisation would advance greatly. That is a prediction for the future.

"It is important to identify people well. In that way you can support them and help them. But giving everyone a blanket method of teaching as if they are all part of a factory of clones really is failing on many, many levels."

Paddina Cole

The Balanced Child

(From a lecture by the spirit of Paddina 17th April 2020)

So, the title for this evening is 'The Balanced Child' and I chose this subject because it is the purpose of all education, both in spirit and of the Earth, that a child, a spirit, a person should be in balance. Without this there are problems, and these problems can cause mental disorders, criminality, abusive and aggressive behaviour and, of course, all the flaws of the Earth that then may very well become extreme, causing further problems. So, ultimately, it is the essential desire, or should be, for all teachers, tutors, professors of education to endeavour, as much as possible, to lead and direct a child towards maintaining a spiritual balance. And this is essential for your future World as much as it has been in the past, neglected at times by the educational aims of the authorities of all countries who expect their children to develop into mature, well behaved and educated adults.

Now, may I say at this point, that achieving balance is difficult but can be achieved and should be expected to be achieved, because balance is far more important, far more, than academic prowess, which possibly achieves nothing other than a memory bank of facts and figures which have their use, of course, but balance and being in a state of balance is the ultimate attainment that all forms of education should endeavour to achieve.

Without balance there is chaos. Without balance there are just many, many possible outcomes, some of which I touched on at the beginning of this discussion this evening. So, how does an educational establishment or directive achieve this? First and foremost, as has been suggested already by these talks, it is that academic subjects are put aside, postponed for a future time when the child has reached a stage of maturity and balance whereby they are then fit and able and willing to adopt lessons of this nature.

So, to start with, by aiming to achieve balance one must be taught and led to understand basic principles and values of a spiritual nature. This is what is essential. This will be the core of the structure of that person and will lead to a balanced state. And this is not, and I repeat, not a form of education which is dictated to an audience of children, demanding that they should learn and remember all that they are given. No. It is offered in a way so that all the children in the class understand and are content to accept what is being given and, if not, then it must be discussed and put to these young minds what is correct and how it should be understood to be correct. And that will continue until all those present have an equal appreciation and understanding of what is required. That is the first stage. And that is going to take time. And, again, it should not be that someone in authority is dictating how long this should take or under what circumstance. It will be for the individual tutor, having been tutored themselves in understanding spiritual values and having been taught, let us call it, the science of spirit, so that they are well tutored in the subject and they will give this so that at the end of the day all children involved in this exercise are agreeable and ready to proceed to the next stage.

Further on from this, children will be taught more about the spiritual structure of their being as well as the physical structure. And over time, much will be explained to them so that they can start to identify which part of them is their physical self and which part of them is their spiritual self. And, by identifying the difference between the two, they will bring the two together as one. That then is the essential foundation for them developing further. By coming to a better understanding of themselves this way and identifying the spiritual being in others, and by further tuition, they will come to understand more about themselves and their true self; very, very important.

It has been said so many times, by so many philosophers and great thinkers of your World, "Get to know thine ownself"; so important. Now, without doing that, it is not possible to maintain balance, spiritual balance. It is a requirement, first and foremost, that all the children and the educational system will endeavour to achieve this state of being to then enable the children to develop into a balanced, mature person. It will be essential.

That is the basic aim for the new educational system which is being proposed here and will come into being because it makes sense. It is how spirit are taught at Home and it should be how spirit, as humanoids on the Earth, will need to be taught as well. Having then reached this state of balance at a certain age and then being prepared for a stage of their education where children in your time now would be considered to be moving on to a secondary education, it will be at this stage that children will be offered academic subjects for them to choose and to start their, let us say, formal academic learning. But, you see, to be in a fit state of mind, having learnt to know themselves so well by then that a child will know the subjects that they would choose and wish to take forward, they would certainly know the subjects that would not be fitting, even if they had not or did not know which subjects to choose entirely. And, of course, there would be tutors well tutored in this way to be there to support the child and help them in their choosing of the subjects they then follow. And those tutors will be very adept spiritually in understanding others because they would have been tutored, in turn, spiritually, having achieved a high level of understanding of themselves, them ownselves, sufficiently well to then have a strong ability to appraise the content and structure of another.

And, of course, in the future, there will be those more in touch with spirit than people of your Earth at this time. So, if advice was needed, it could be called upon with this work, and spirit will be available to do this. That is for the future, but meanwhile, what is being proposed here is a revolution in education and it is going to need a lot of grounded tuition to begin with for tutors to then go forward, and this will take time. But, nonetheless, the seeds of this system of education have been sown since Erasmus started talking and teaching back in the late seventies and early eighties.

And this will be a revolution, quiet, peaceful, but so much is to change. So much is required to change. When we look at the difficulties and the challenges that children face in primary school, I think of all those things we have discussed, and there may be more we haven't discussed, but all of this illustrates very well the imbalance within the World, because the imbalance starts with Mankind, and therefore, it must begin with the children of Mankind who are to be the responsible parents for tomorrow and tomorrow's World.

The Seven Ages of Man

(From a lecture by the spirit of Paddina 24th April 2020)

The subject we have for this evening is 'The Seven Ages of Man'. Now, why have I introduced this in accordance with our programme for children's education? Well, I would offer to you that this really means that education starts the very second you enter the Earth as a child and continues right through to the time when, according to your Tapestry, your life would end within the Earth and you as a spirit then return Home to my land from whence you came originally. So that is the seven ages of Man on the Earth. But also the education doesn't finish there of course. It is when we are at Home in spirit, having understood and experienced all that was within the Earth, we have the added opportunity and ability, using our minds with greater clarity at Home, that we can then analyse the purpose of the life, its meaning, the choices we made where we did well, or where we did not so well, and we have a good understanding of all of this.

Now, it is not essential for a child to have that appreciation of why he or she is living a life at that age, but later when they are more adult then perhaps it would be of interest. In times in the future it will be seen and understood that the education does not finish during the time of schooling, because it will be a spiritual education, meaning that all purpose of life, all things that happen within a life are to teach and thereby for all to learn; that is the purpose of life, that is why you are here, you are here to learn in the University of Life, Eritha.

So, you would understand if we take the seven ages of Man we will see the first is up until the age of 10, primary education, and we have talked on this, and I have proffered some proposals for how teaching for this age could be in the future and how it would benefit all if, I believe, my proposal was to be accepted within the Earth. We shall see how Mankind views this aspect of education given by spirit, myself.

We then come on to the second stage, or let us say the second age of Man, which is, of course, the secondary education where, because of the nature of life within the Earth, Man must learn more academic subjects to suit the nature of people's interests and ambitions for making themselves a career and a purpose within the life. And, again, this would be directed in accordance with how their Tapestry was designed that this person should follow a certain path. This would be investigated, interpreted and understood by those on the Earth; perhaps, in the beginnings, with spiritual guidance to help make this happen.

And then we come to the third age where the person is beginning to prepare a career, even perhaps thoughts of a partnership and a family, a relationship. This is how life evolves traditionally within the Earth. Again, in accordance with the structure of people within the Earth and also not only the individual Tapestry but the Overall Tapestry directs people to follow in this way. And it is at this stage, again thinking about the future when there will be more, let us say, intensity of study, according to that person's interest, yes, and the nature of the work they are to do and have started doing, but more importantly people of that time will show more interest, more curiosity, more intrigue, more desire to learn both spiritually and in accordance with nature and the Natural Law. This is how it is to be, which of course is initiated by the primary education in the very beginning which opens up a child's eye and vision of the World and all it contains. And this will inspire curiosity and interest in all that is offered within the life on Earth.

With the following age of Man, the fourth, which is between 30 and 40, this is a time very often where a person's life, their Tapestry, there is change, there is a different direction offered, there are many things that might happen at that time, and again, if it is so, this will be analysed and understood more with spiritual education and understanding than people of your time do now. So for the future, for how a person negotiates their life and goes forward, perhaps after a freedom of choice in the life, there will be much greater education and understanding spiritually which will help them and give them some greater appreciation of why these things occur and why the Tapestry has made it so for that person to learn by. It will be further understood.

So then, if we go to the fifth age, between 40 and 50, yes things perhaps are slowing down a little in some ways but, again, whatever happens in that life, whatever challenges and tests reveal themselves from within the Tapestry, again there will be change, as throughout the life there are times of change as it must be, as it should be, it will be and, again, the education for the future, not Mankind now, no, he is not ready, he is not taught, he does not know sufficient to have the realisation that yet again a change in life, different things that develop, are meant to be and are meant to test that person and to give them something to learn by.

And between 50 and 60, yes, again more so perhaps, the body is not quite so capable as it was when it was younger, stronger and fitter but by now there is the beginning of an understanding, perhaps developing a certain wisdom; and by the seventh age, between 60 and 70 and on-going, as the body quietens, as there is more time and space and that time of life allows for more thinking, more observation, perhaps more reflection on what has happened, this gives a person a greater wisdom and understanding.

That is the fulfilment, and for some, not all, but for some, that will be the fruition, the fruiting of the life, to have worked hard throughout that life, to finally come to some sense of achievement and understanding, perhaps even gifted with the fruit of those years, blossoming into some fulfilment, which again is the meaning and the purpose of life revealed.

So that is, in its simplicity, an explanation of how I would demonstrate the seven ages of Man, not Spirit, of Man. It is simplistic but, having said that, it does express that there are certain times within the person's life, ongoing, where there are changes and developments and where there is a metamorphosis from one stage, one time, one age through to another, all with purpose, meaningful, and for good reason, and that is the education. The education for Man.

Now, I would suggest it is important that children at school have some understanding of this so that they can go forward with more appreciation of their spiritual self and its purpose and how life is to lead them forward into new experiences and new lessons of life.

I would suggest also, as I think it has been mentioned before, that this spiritual understanding, this spiritual tuition afforded to the young, as it will be, is more essential in creating a solid and profound foundation for that person's life, for all children's lives, what they go on to, so that the academic subjects they choose at a later time will be fitting in accordance with a very well founded understanding of how their life is to be directed. The academic tuition will be, almost, simply a part of life but not as important as the spiritual tuition which will be on-going throughout their life. I am not suggesting that people in the future will be attending school throughout their life, of course not, this will not be necessary, but there will be times when perhaps there are priests, a priesthood, male, female, those who will be at a particular centre, let us say, a branch of the Foundation, where if a person needs guidance and a little help in understanding themselves, their life and others, then they will be free to approach someone. So, yes, that is how the education will continue, as it has been for this Foundation, perhaps not quite so, let us say, intense as it has been for those within the Foundation here, but nonetheless this will be a model for the future and how it will be. There will be those who will be well tutored, who will be selected and chosen to do this work, they will have that understanding and they would gladly accept; and if it is possible that the person having been offered this gift would refuse it, or for whatever reason move away into another direction, then so be it, there will always be someone to maintain the role of priesthood and tutorship in every country where there is a Foundation of The Erasmus Foundation; so it will be. And, again, of course, nothing will be demanded of anyone, these branches will be there to offer assistance and help as it may be required, but no-one will be told or demanded in any way that they should do this or that, it would be most wrong and would not be acceptable.

But education for the future is to take on, I would say, a different role, a different meaning, perhaps a more profound meaning in that the purpose and the results of such an education will be fundamental, greater in its content and its effect and teaching on the individual, leading to a greater appreciation of life and all it contains. It should make people more peaceful. I would say, generally speaking, people will be more content, they will see life with greater purpose for them to enjoy and to welcome the challenges and tests in life as something that has been given to them to experience and work through. All of that will be understood. It will give people so much more. There will be less fear, certainly less fear of death, there will be more appreciation of the natural world, nature, and the creatures and all that it contains. So much to enjoy and, may I say, it will be a little 'heaven on Earth', but the education has to start quite soon with the young; and so it will be.

"Of course any science student can tell us more about nature and her laws than can Descartes or Newton - but what can he tell us about the human spirit?"

Antoine de Saint-Exupéry